AF446502

The Phase Into Retirement™
Field Guide

—The—
PHASE
Into Retirement™
FIELD GUIDE

Your 5-Step Roadmap to Purpose, Health, Activities, Social Connection & Everyday Joy in Retirement

PurposeNext

© 2026 PurposeNext

All rights reserved. No part of this publication may be reproduced, stored in a retrieval system or transmitted in any form or by any means – electronic, mechanical, photocopying, recording or otherwise – without prior written consent from the publisher, except for the inclusion of brief quotations in a review.

For more information about this title or to order additional copies, contact the publisher: hello@purposenext.com.

Manufactured in the United States of America

ISBN 979-8-9860067-2-7 (paperback)

Retire With Purpose. Thrive With Clarity.

PHASE Into Retirement™ is a practical, research-informed framework designed to help people prepare for the life side of retirement—not just the financial side. Built around five essential dimensions—Purpose, Health, Activities, Social Life, and Everyday Life—PHASE helps individuals understand how these interconnected elements shape well-being, satisfaction, and momentum after work ends. This booklet translates decades of research into clear insights and reflections that help readers intentionally design a retirement marked by meaning, connection, structure, and joy.

Purpose

Health

Activities

Social Life

Everyday Life

PHASE helps individuals understand how these interconnected elements shape well-being, satisfaction, and momentum after work ends. This booklet translates decades of research into clear insights and reflections that help readers intentionally design a retirement marked by meaning, connection, structure, and joy.

This Field Guide can be used on its own, but you'll get far more value from it when paired with your personal PHASE Into Retirement™ assessment results.

To unlock the full experience—and make these insights truly relevant to your life—visit PHASEIntoRetirement.com and complete your assessment. It takes less than fifteen minutes, and it will bring sharper clarity, deeper meaning, and more direction to everything that follows.

For more information about this title or to order additional copies, contact the publisher: hello@purposenext.com

PHASE

Into Retirement™

DESIGNING THE LIFE YOU DESERVE

Retirement is not an ending — it's the most exciting redesign project of your life. For decades, someone else's calendar shaped your days. Now, for the first time, you hold the pen. That freedom is extraordinary — and it deserves to be met with intention.

Research is clear: the retirees who thrive aren't the ones who simply stopped working — they're the ones who actively designed what came next. They built new rhythms, rekindled curiosity, deepened connections, and found fresh ways to matter. That's exactly what this work will help you do.

The PHASE™ framework addresses the five dimensions that
determine whether retirement flourishes or fades:
Purpose • Health • Activities • Social Life • Everyday Life

These five pillars don't work in isolation — they reinforce one another. Purpose fuels movement. Movement opens doors to new activities. Activities spark friendships. Friendships build daily rhythm. And daily rhythm deepens your sense of who you are. When even one pillar strengthens, the others rise with it.

The Work Ahead — and Why It's Worth It

The pages that follow will ask you to reflect, to dig, and to dream. You'll be invited to examine your values, your habits, your relationships, and your routines — not to judge them, but to **build on them.** Some questions will feel easy. Others may surprise you. All of them are worth your honest attention.

This is not a test — there are no wrong answers. But there is a direct relationship between what you put in and what you get out. **The richer your reflection, the more powerful your plan.** Approach this as a gift to your future self — a few focused hours that could shape the next 20 or 30 years.

You cannot accidentally create the retirement you want.
But you can intentionally design it — and it starts right here.

P — PURPOSE

Reimagining Who You Are When Work No Longer Defines You

> **Your Purpose (P) Score**
> Look back at your **P score** from the PHASE™ assessment. A strong score suggests you already have meaningful direction beyond work. A lower score simply means this chapter may unlock some of the most important discoveries ahead. Either way, this is where the next chapter of meaning begins.

Here's the truth about retirement that most people don't see coming: **when work ends, so does the built-in answer to one of life's most important questions — "Who am I?"**

For decades, your job gave you an identity. It told you where to go, what to do, and how you mattered. Even if you didn't love every minute of it, work gave your days shape and your life direction. When that structure is gone, it's completely normal to feel a mix of relief and disorientation. That's not a sign something is wrong. That's a sign you're human.

The good news? Purpose doesn't disappear when you retire. It just needs to be rebuilt — on your own terms, in your own way. It might be quieter than your career purpose. More personal. Less about what others expect of you and more about what truly lights you up. Mentoring someone. Caring for grandchildren. Volunteering for a cause that matters to you. Learning something you've always wanted to learn. There is no single right answer — only your answer.

What the PHASE™ assessment was looking at goes deeper than you might expect. It wasn't simply asking whether you feel purposeful — it was probing the specific sources that research shows actually sustain purpose in retirement. Do you draw meaning from helping and contributing to others, not just from paid work? Does your family give your life direction and significance? Do you volunteer — and do it regularly enough to build real connection and routine around it? Do you see yourself as someone who keeps learning and growing, or has that drive faded? Are you worried about who you'll be when work no longer defines you, or do you feel ready? A strong P score means those sources are already active in your life. A lower score is a signal that retirement may arrive before those foundations are in place — and this chapter is designed to help you build them before that happens.

What the research is clear on: **people who retire with a strong sense of purpose live longer, stay healthier, think more sharply, and feel more satisfied with their lives.** Purpose isn't just a nice idea. It's fuel. It gets you out of bed in the morning and keeps you moving forward. But it doesn't just appear. It takes reflection. It takes honesty. It takes trying new things and paying attention to what energizes you. The work you do in these pages is exactly that kind of effort — and it is absolutely worth it.

YOUR PURPOSE REFLECTION

Take your time with each question. Your most honest answers will give you the most useful results.

1. **Think of a time in your life — at work or elsewhere — when you felt fully alive and engaged. What were you doing that made that moment feel so meaningful?**

This is your personal benchmark for what purpose feels like.

My answer:

____

____

____

____

____

2. **What do people come to me for? What do my family, friends, or colleagues count on me to do, know, or provide?**

Sometimes our purpose hides in plain sight — in the ways we already show up for others. List as many things as come to mind, big and small. These are clues to the contribution you're naturally wired to make.

My answer:

____

____

____

____

3. **What topics, causes, or activities have I always been drawn to — even if I never had enough time to explore them?**

The PHASE™ assessment specifically measured whether you volunteer, help others outside of work, and actively seek to learn new things — because those three behaviors are among the most powerful predictors of sustained purpose in retirement. If volunteering, teaching, mentoring, or learning something new comes to mind here, pay attention to that. Those aren't just hobbies. They are proven on-ramps to a purposeful life.

My answer:

____

____

____

____

4. **When I imagine my ideal Tuesday in retirement — a completely ordinary day — what does it look like? Who am I with? What am I doing? How do I feel at the end of it?**

Be specific. A fulfilling retirement is built from ordinary days that feel worth living, not just big moments. The assessment asked whether you worry about your purpose when work ends — this question is your chance to replace that worry with a clear, personal vision of what a meaningful day actually looks like for you.

My answer:

____

____

____

____

____

5. **Looking at my answers above, what themes or patterns do I notice? What kinds of activities, people, or contributions keep showing up?**

Look for the thread that connects your answers. Do you keep coming back to teaching, creating, serving, exploring, connecting? That pattern is not random. It's the shape of your purpose trying to make itself known. Name it.

My answer:

____

____

____

____

____

6. **Using what I've written in this section, complete these three things:**

First — My identity statement

"I am someone who _____."

Don't describe what you plan to do. Describe who you are becoming. This is the foundation everything else is built on.

My identity statement:

____

____

Second — My first step, with a day and time

My first concrete step toward purpose in retirement is ____, and I will do it on [day] at [time].

Without a specific day and time, "soon" almost always means never. Lock it in now.

My first step and when I will do it:

____

____

Third — My accountability person

The person I will tell about this commitment is ____, because they will help me follow through.

You don't need to make it a big conversation. A text, an email, or one sentence over dinner is enough. Saying it out loud to someone makes it real.

The person I will tell and what I will ask them:

____

____

Purpose is not found. It is formed —
piece by piece, choice by choice, day by day.

H — HEALTH

Taking Care of the Body and Mind That Will Carry You Through Retirement

> **Your Health (H) Score**
>
> Take a look at your **H score** from the PHASE™ assessment. A higher score shows that your habits and mindset are supporting your long-term vitality. A lower score signals that this chapter may contain some of the most powerful improvements you can make. Wherever you're starting, the choices ahead can change everything.

Here is something most people don't fully appreciate until they retire: **your health is not just a personal concern — it is the engine that powers everything else.**

When your energy is good, retirement opens up. You travel. You stay active. You show up fully for the people you love. When health struggles, even things you're excited about can start to feel out of reach. Health is what makes the rest of your retirement plan possible.

The encouraging truth is this: the choices you make right now — before or in the early days of retirement — have an outsized impact on how the years ahead feel. Small, consistent habits matter far more than dramatic overhauls. A daily walk. Better sleep. One appointment you've been putting off. These are not small things. They are the foundation.

What the PHASE™ assessment was looking at is worth understanding clearly. It wasn't just asking whether you're healthy in a general sense — it was asking specific questions that reveal how health is already affecting your retirement readiness. Are there physical limitations that stop you from doing activities you want to do, like hiking, pickleball, or cycling? Does your health get in the way of everyday tasks at home? Have mobility issues caused you to miss trips or visits with family and friends? Do you feel anxious on a regular basis, or find yourself losing interest in things you used to enjoy? How optimistic are you that your health will allow you to live the retirement you're hoping for? And do you already have habits and routines in place — or are you relying on motivation you'll need to build from scratch? These questions matter because the gap between the retirement you want and the one you'll actually have often comes down to health. A strong H score means you're already closing that gap. A lower score means there's meaningful work to do — and the best time to start is now, not at retirement.

You don't need to become someone who loves the gym or follows a perfect diet. **You just need to become someone who takes their health seriously and makes small, steady choices that add up.** Research shows that people who approach retirement with strong health habits — and a positive mindset about aging — stay more active, more engaged, and more satisfied with life for decades longer than those who don't. The questions below will help you figure out exactly what that looks like for you.

YOUR HEALTH REFLECTION

These questions are designed to build on one another. Read through all of them once before you start writing, then go back and answer each one. Your answers will carry forward — by the end, you'll have everything you need to make a clear, personal health commitment.

1. **Describe a time in my life when I felt genuinely well — physically energetic and mentally clear. What was I doing differently during that time?**

Think about your sleep, your movement, your stress level, your eating, your social life. What stands out as different about how you were living then? This doesn't have to be recent — even a season from years ago counts. This is your personal benchmark for what feeling well actually feels like for you.

My answer:

____

____

____

____

____

____

2.   **What is honestly getting in the way of my health right now — and what story am I telling myself that makes it easy to stay stuck?**

Be as honest as you can here. For some people, the obstacle is a real physical limitation — pain, mobility, a condition that makes certain activities hard. That is real, and it matters. For others, the obstacle is more about motivation, time, or a story like "I'll start Monday" or "it won't make a difference at my age." Most of us have a little of both. Name whatever is true for you — you can't work around something you haven't named.

My answer:

____

____

____

____

____

____

3.   **Five years into retirement, I want to be able to _______. To do that, my health needs to look like _______.**

The PHASE™ assessment asked whether health issues stop you from doing physical activities — things like hiking, pickleball, cycling — or from taking trips and visiting family and friends. Those aren't abstract questions. They are about the actual experiences that make retirement worth living. What do you want your body and mind to be able to do? That's your 'why,' and it matters more than any specific habit.

My answer:

____

____

____

____

____

4. **What is a healthy habit I have successfully kept before, even briefly? What made it stick that time?**

You have more evidence of what works for you than you might think. It might be a stretch when you walked every day for a month, a period when you slept well, or a season when your anxiety was lower because of something specific you were doing. Look for the conditions that made it happen — a friend, a schedule, a clear reason. Those conditions are clues to what will work again.

My answer:

____

____

____

____

____

5. **Looking back at my answers above, if I could only change one thing about how I am caring for my health right now, what one change would have the biggest ripple effect on everything else?**

Not a list — just one thing. The assessment asked about anxiety, loss of interest in daily life, physical limitations, and optimism about the future. For many people, the single biggest lever is movement — even a short daily walk improves sleep, reduces anxiety, lifts mood, and builds confidence. For others it's sleep, or stress, or finally addressing a physical issue they've been avoiding. What is the one change that unlocks the others for you?

My answer:

____

____

____

____

____

6. Using what I've written in this section, complete these three things:

First — My identity statement

"I am someone who takes care of their health by _____."

Not "I want to" or "I plan to." I am. The shift from intention to identity is where lasting change begins.

My identity statement:

____

____

Second — My first step, with a day and time

The one health change I am starting with is _____, and I will do it for the first time on [day] at [time].

Without a specific day and time, "soon" almost always means never. Lock it in now.

My first step and when I will do it:

____

____

Third — My accountability person

The person I will tell about this health commitment is _____, because _____.

Choose someone who will actually ask you about it — not just someone who will say "that's great." A little healthy pressure goes a long way.

The person I will tell and what I will ask them:

____

____

You don't have to be perfect. You just have to be intentional.

Taking your health seriously is one of the most generous things you can do — for yourself and for everyone who loves you.

A — ACTIVITIES

The Engagement, Curiosity, and Creativity That Bring Retirement to Life

> **Your Activities (A) Score**
> Think back to your **A score**. This score reflects how engaged your life outside of work currently is — your hobbies, interests, and willingness to explore new pursuits. A high score means you already have momentum. A lower score means there's a wide horizon of new experiences waiting to be discovered.

Here is what surprises most new retirees: rest feels wonderful for a few weeks, and then it starts to feel like something else. **Without engagement, rest turns into drift. And drift is one of the quietest threats to a happy retirement.**

The retirees who describe their lives as full, exciting, and meaningful are rarely the ones who rested the most. They are the ones who stayed engaged — with hobbies, curiosities, creative projects, causes, classes, and communities. They used retirement not to withdraw from life, but to rediscover the parts of themselves that work had pushed to the margins.

Activities are not filler. They are the architecture of a meaningful day. They give you something to anticipate, something to practice, something to improve at, and something to share. Research is clear: retirees who actively engage in hobbies and interests are significantly less likely to experience depression, more likely to stay socially connected, and far more likely to describe retirement as thriving rather than just getting by.

What the PHASE™ assessment looked at is important to understand. It wasn't just asking whether you have hobbies — it was asking whether your activities leave you feeling energized, whether you pursue them consistently across the year rather than only in certain seasons, whether they help you manage stress, and whether you're genuinely open to exploring new things. A rich activity life has both depth — a few things you do well and often — and breadth — curiosity about what else might be out there.

The good news: **it is never too late to build this.** Engagement can be built from scratch at any age. You don't need to find a passion overnight. You just need to follow small sparks of curiosity — a class you've thought about, a group you've noticed, something you loved before work took over. The brain thrives on novelty and challenge at every age. The only thing standing between you and a more engaged retirement is the first small step.

The questions below are designed to help you take that step with intention. They will help you identify what already energizes you, what you've been curious about, where the gaps in your current activity life are, and what a truly engaged week might look like for you. Work through them honestly — the richness of your answers is directly proportional to the richness of the plan you'll walk away with.

YOUR ACTIVITIES REFLECTION

These questions build on one another. Read through all of them once before you start writing, then go back and answer each one. By the end, you'll have a clear, personal picture of what an engaged retirement looks like for you.

1. **Think about the activities, hobbies, or interests I already have — the things I do outside of work and daily chores. Which ones leave me feeling most energized and alive when I'm done?**

Don't just list them — think about why those particular ones light you up. Is it the creativity? The physical challenge? The people you do it with? The sense of getting better at something? The answers here are clues to what kind of engagement matters most to you.

My answer:

____

____

____

____

____

____

2. **What activities or interests did I enjoy earlier in my life that I've set aside — and what is one thing I've always been curious about but never made time to try?**

Think back before your career consumed most of your time and energy. These could be things from your 20s or 30s, a class you've thought about, a skill you've admired in others, or something that catches your eye in a magazine or conversation. Dormant interests are not dead ones — they're waiting.

My answer:

____

____

____

____

____

____

3. **Honestly, how much of my current activity life is seasonal, narrow, or dependent on one or two things that could easily disappear?**

The PHASE™ assessment specifically looked at whether hobbies are year-round or only seasonal, and how many hours a week you actually spend on activities you choose. If most of your engagement is tied to one season, one sport, or one activity, retirement could leave some very long gaps. Where are the gaps in your current activity life, and what types of activities — physical, creative, social, intellectual — are missing?

My answer:

____

____

____

____

____

____

4. **When I picture a truly great, ordinary week in retirement — not a vacation, just a regular week — what kinds of activities fill it? What am I doing, learning, creating, or contributing?**

Be as specific as you can. A fulfilling retirement is built from engaged ordinary weeks, not just big moments. Think about the mix: something physical, something creative or intellectual, something social, something that involves learning or getting better. What does your ideal engaged week actually look like?

My answer:

5. **What is one activity I've been curious about that I could try in the next 30 days — in a small, low-stakes way — just to see if it sparks something?**

You don't need to commit to anything. The PHASE™ assessment asked whether you've recently tried new activities and whether you're open to experimenting in retirement — because the retirees who build rich activity lives are the ones willing to show up as a beginner and see what happens. One class, one meetup, one YouTube tutorial. What is the smallest possible version of something new you could try?

My answer:

6. **Using what I've written in this section, complete these three things:**

First — My identity statement

"I am someone who stays curious and engaged. In retirement, that looks like ____."

This isn't about listing hobbies. It's about claiming an identity — the kind of person who shows up for life, tries new things, and keeps growing.

My identity statement:

____

____

Second — My first step, with a day and time

The first activity I am going to try or return to is ____, and I will take one concrete step toward it on [day] at [time].

Without a specific day and time, "soon" almost always means never. Lock it in now.

My first step and when I will do it:

____

____

Third — My accountability person

The person I will tell about this is ____, and what I'll ask them is ____.

Maybe you'll ask them to join you. Maybe you'll just ask them to check in. Either way, saying it out loud to someone turns a private intention into a real commitment.

The person I will tell and what I will ask them:

____

____

Activities are rarely accidental. They are invitations — small moments of curiosity that grow into life-giving practices.

Your next chapter is waiting. All it needs is your curiosity and a first step.

S — SOCIAL LIFE

Connection, Belonging, and the Friendships That Shape a Joyful Retirement

Your Social Life (S) Score
Recall your **S score** from the PHASE™ assessment. A strong score suggests you already have meaningful relationships beyond the workplace. A lower score simply highlights an opportunity to strengthen one of the most powerful drivers of happiness in retirement: connection.

Of all the things that shape how happy retirement feels, social connection is the one most people underestimate — until it's gone. **Research consistently finds that the quality of your relationships matters more to retirement satisfaction than almost anything else, including money.**

Here is what most people don't see coming: work does more than pay the bills. It gives you a social life. Colleagues, clients, meetings, shared projects, coffee conversations — for decades, your job placed you around people every single day. When work ends, that community can disappear faster than you expect. Not because those people didn't matter, but because most work friendships are held together by proximity and shared routine — two things that vanish the moment you retire.

What the PHASE™ assessment was looking at goes deeper than simply asking how many friends you have. It was asking questions that reveal how sturdy your social life really is. What fraction of your friendships exist only inside work — and how many would survive without it? If family wasn't available, could a friend step in to help with something physical, or hold space for a hard conversation? After a draining week, do you turn toward people or away from them? How often do you actually reach out to friends, not just intend to? And are you satisfied — not just with how many friends you have, but with how deeply those friendships go? A high S score means your social foundation is already strong and diverse. A lower score is a signal worth taking seriously: it means retirement could arrive before the friendships are in place to sustain you — and the best time to build them is now, while life still provides some natural structure to build around.

The good news is this: **social connection can be built at any age, and it doesn't require a large personality or a packed calendar.** It requires showing up consistently, being willing to be known, and placing yourself in environments where friendship can grow naturally over time. The questions below are designed to help you take stock of where you are, remember what rich connection has felt like in your life, and build a clear plan for the social life you want in retirement.

YOUR SOCIAL LIFE REFLECTION

These questions build on one another. Read through all of them once before you start writing, then go back and answer each one. By the end, you'll have a clear picture of the social life you want — and a concrete plan to build it.

1. **Think back to a time in my life when my social life felt genuinely rich — when I felt connected, known, and glad to be around the people in my life. What was different about that time?**

Think about the friendships themselves, but also the circumstances. Were you part of a community, a team, a group? Were you showing up somewhere regularly? Were you in a season of life that made connection easier? What you describe here is your personal picture of what a healthy social life looks and feels like for you.

My answer:

____

____

____

____

____

____

2. **If I'm honest, how many of my current friendships exist mainly because of work — and how many would survive if work disappeared tomorrow?**

The PHASE™ assessment asked specifically what fraction of your friends are work friends and how likely you are to stay in touch with them after retirement. This is not a judgment — it's a reality check. Work friendships are real and valuable, but most don't survive the transition. Which of your current friendships are built on something deeper than shared office space? Name the ones that would last.

My answer:

____

____

____

____

____

3. **If I needed real help — not just company, but actual support, either physically or emotionally — which friends could I call? And are there gaps I notice?**

The PHASE™ assessment asked two pointed questions: whether a friend could help you with a physical task if family wasn't available, and whether a friend could hold a hard, sensitive conversation with you. Those aren't small asks. They describe a friendship that has real depth and trust. Who in your life fits that description? And where do you notice the gaps — people you enjoy but couldn't lean on that way?

My answer:

____

____

____

____

____

4. **After a hard or exhausting week, do I tend to reach toward people or pull away from them — and what does that tell me about what I need from my social life in retirement?**

The assessment asked whether you'd want to spend time with friends after a stressful week — and how often you proactively reach out to people, not just respond when others initiate. There's no wrong answer here. Some people are restored by company; others need solitude first. But the pattern matters. If you tend to pull away when life gets hard, retirement's quieter rhythms can make isolation easier to drift into than you might expect. What does a social life that genuinely restores you look like?

My answer:

____

____

____

____

____

5. **Looking at what I've written, what is the most important gap in my social life right now — and what is one environment, group, or relationship I could invest in to begin closing it?**

The assessment asked whether you're satisfied with both the number of friends in your life and the quality of those friendships — because both matter. You might have plenty of people but feel that the connections are shallow. Or you might have one or two deep friendships but worry about what happens if they change. Name the gap honestly. Then name one place — a group, a class, a community, a specific person — where you could begin building what's missing. The smaller and more specific, the better.

My answer:

____

____

____

____

____

6.   Using what I've written in this section, complete these three things:

First — My identity statement

"I am someone who invests in friendship. In retirement, that looks like _____."

Social connection doesn't happen by accident in retirement — it happens by decision. This statement is your declaration that you're someone who chooses connection, not just someone who hopes for it.

My identity statement:

____

____

Second — My first step, with a day and time

The first step I will take to build or deepen my social life is _____, and I will do it on [day] at [time].

Without a specific day and time, "soon" almost always means never. Lock it in now.

My first step and when I will do it:

____

____

Third — My accountability person

The person I will tell about this commitment is _____, and what I'll ask them is _____.

The accountability person for your social life might be the same person you're trying to connect with more. Or it might be someone who knows you well enough to ask the hard question: "Did you actually do it?"

The person I will tell and what I will ask them:

____

____

Retirement may remove the social scaffolding of work, but it offers something better: the chance to build a social life based entirely on choice.

You are not meant to face retirement alone. The people who will make it joyful are out there — and so are you.

E — EVERYDAY LIFE

The Rhythm, Stability, and Structure That Keep Retirement Grounded

> **Your Everyday Life (E) Score**
> Consider your **E score**. This reflects how much structure, rhythm, and intention currently shape your days. A high score means you already have routines that work. A lower score means this chapter will help you design the daily patterns that make retirement feel purposeful rather than drifting.

O f all the things retirement changes, this one catches people off guard most: **when work ends, so does the structure that organized your days. And without structure, even the best intentions for retirement begin to drift.**

During your working years, structure was built into your life whether you thought about it or not. Your alarm went off. Meetings were scheduled. Deadlines gave the week shape. Lunch happened at predictable times. Your evenings organized themselves around the demands of the next morning. You may not have loved all of it — but it worked. When that scaffolding disappears overnight, what's left is wide-open time that can feel like freedom for a few weeks, and then quietly like drift.

What the PHASE™ assessment was looking at is worth understanding. It wasn't just asking whether you're an organized person — it was probing something more specific and more telling. One of the most important things it measured was the gap between how well you manage your time at work versus how well you manage your time at home. Many people are excellent at work time management — because work imposes the structure for them. But when asked how well they manage time at home, the number drops. That gap is the retirement risk. It means the structure you've been relying on has been coming from outside you, not from within. The assessment also asked whether a completely free weekend makes you reach for a plan or relax into the unknown, whether you already have a picture of what your retirement days and weeks will look like, and whether the loss of work structure genuinely worries you. Those questions together reveal something important: not whether you like structure, but whether you know how to build it for yourself.

The happiest retirees are not the busiest ones. **They are the ones who build routines that give their days a shape they actually enjoy — routines that fit who they are, not routines borrowed from a job.** Structure in retirement doesn't mean filling every hour. It means having enough rhythm in your days and weeks that you feel grounded, purposeful, and in motion. The questions below will help you figure out what that looks like for you — drawing on seasons of your life when your routines actually worked, and building toward a clear picture of the daily and weekly rhythms you want to carry into retirement.

YOUR EVERYDAY LIFE REFLECTION

These questions build on one another. Read through all of them once before you start writing, then go back and answer each one. By the end, you'll have a clear picture of the daily and weekly rhythms that will keep your retirement grounded and moving forward.

1. **Think back to a season of my life when my daily routine felt genuinely good — when I felt grounded, productive, and in control of my time. What did that rhythm look like?**

This doesn't have to be recent. It might be a period during a particular job, a time when your household was running well, or even a stretch of a few months when you felt on top of things. Think about what time you woke up, what you did first, how your day flowed. What made that rhythm feel sustainable and satisfying rather than pressured or chaotic?

My answer:

____

____

____

____

____

____

2. **Honestly, how much of my current daily structure comes from work — and what does my time actually look like when work isn't organizing it for me?**

The PHASE™ assessment asked separately how well you manage time at work and how well you manage time at home — because those two answers are often very different. Work imposes structure whether you're naturally organized or not. Home time is different: no one schedules it for you, and no deadline forces you to use it well. Think about weekends, vacations, or any long stretch without a work schedule. What does your time look like when it's completely your own? What drifts, and what stays steady?

My answer:

____

____

____

____

____

3.   **When I have a completely unscheduled day or weekend — no appointments, no obligations — what is my honest first reaction, and what does the time usually end up looking like?**

The assessment asked whether a free weekend makes you reach for a to-do list or let the day unfold. Neither is wrong — but both reveal something about what you'll need in retirement. If a free day energizes you, retirement's open calendar will likely feel like a gift. If a free day makes you restless, anxious, or unproductive, retirement's wide-open time will need more intentional design than you might expect. What does your honest pattern tell you?

My answer:

____

____

____

____

____

4. **If I could design my ideal retirement day and week from scratch — not a vacation, but a real, sustainable ordinary week — what would it look like?**

Think about what time you'd wake up and what you'd do first. The PHASE™ assessment asked whether you already have a picture of what your retirement days and weeks will look like — because retirees who go in with even a loose plan adjust far more smoothly than those who don't. You don't need every hour mapped out. But what anchors would your ideal week have? What would happen in the mornings? What would give your week its shape and rhythm?

My answer:

____

____

____

____

____

5. **What is the one thing I am most worried about losing when work no longer organizes my time — and what is one routine or rhythm I could put in place to replace it?**

The assessment asked directly whether the loss of work structure worries you — and whether clutter or disorganization at home tends to affect your mood. If structure disappearing is a real concern for you, that self-awareness is actually a gift: it means you know what you need, and you can design for it. Name the specific thing you're afraid of losing — the morning deadline, the weekly rhythm, the sense of being needed and on task. Then name one concrete routine that could replace it.

My answer:

____

____

____

____

____

6. Using what I've written in this section, complete these three things:

First — My identity statement

"I am someone who creates their own structure. In retirement, my days look like _____."

This is the most important shift in the Everyday Life dimension: from someone whose structure came from a job to someone whose structure comes from within. Claim it. The routine you design for yourself is more sustainable than any schedule a workplace ever gave you.

My identity statement:

____

____

Second — My first step, with a day and time

The first routine I am going to put in place is _____, and I will start it on [day] at [time].

Without a specific day and time, "soon" almost always means never. Lock it in now.

My first step and when I will do it:

____

____

Third — My accountability person

The person I will tell about this routine is _____, and what I'll ask them is _____.

Your accountability person for structure might be a spouse, a friend, or someone who will notice if your mornings start drifting. Pick someone who will ask "How's the routine going?" — and who you'll actually answer honestly.

The person I will tell and what I will ask them:

____

____

Structure is not a cage. It is the ground beneath your feet — the thing that makes everything else in retirement possible.

You built a life around work's rhythm for decades. Now you get to build one around your own.

A Framework for Designing a Life of Meaning, Health, Connection, and Joy

Introduction: Retirement Is a Redesign

Retirement sits in the cultural imagination as both a promise and a paradox. The promise is freedom — an escape from alarm clocks, deadlines, email inboxes, and the perpetual rhythm of obligation. The paradox is what arrives when that freedom actually comes. People spend decades thinking about what they want *less* of: less work, less stress, less pressure, less time spent doing things they didn't choose. But very few spend meaningful time imagining what they want *more* of — more purpose, more connection, more learning, more momentum, more joy.

This is why so many retirees arrive at their first Monday without work and feel two conflicting sensations at once. One is relief. The other is an unexpected and unsettling question: *What now?*

For most people, retirement is the first time since childhood that life becomes unscheduled. From grade school through our last day of employment, we live inside someone else's calendar. Bells ring. Meetings begin. Deadlines loom. Vacations end. Emails pile up. Life is shaped by structures handed to us. Even when we complain about that structure, it nevertheless organizes our days, guides our decisions, and defines our identities.

Removing that structure doesn't just free time — it disturbs a psychological ecosystem that has held your life together for decades. That disruption is not a sign that you've misprepared. It is simply the reality of human nature: we are creatures who thrive on rhythm, connection, movement, meaning, and routine. When the scaffolding that supported those needs is suddenly removed, we must build a new one.

For most of human history, life after work was short. Retirement, as we understand it, barely existed. But now, with longer lifespans and healthier aging, people often spend 20 to 30 years in this chapter. It is too large a part of life to drift through without intention, and too precious a chapter to spend feeling unanchored or disengaged.

That's where PHASE™ comes in. PHASE Into Retirement™ is designed to guide pre-retirees and retirees through the five non-financial dimensions that predict whether retirement becomes a season of flourishing or simply fading. These dimensions are:

Purpose Health Activities Social Life Everyday Life. These elements are not merely categories; they are interdependent forces that shape emotional well-being, physical vitality, and daily satisfaction. They are the architecture of a meaningful life after work — a life shaped not by external expectations, but by your own values, rhythms, and joys.

The PHASE™ model evolved from research across gerontology, psychology, behavioral science, and longitudinal aging studies. It reflects what retirees themselves say in the years and decades after they leave full-time work. Retirement happiness is never rooted in leisure alone. It is built through connection, contribution, curiosity, routine, and movement. It is built through choosing roles that align with who you are becoming, not simply who you used to be.

You cannot "accidentally" create the retirement you want. You must design it — not all at once, but gradually, intentionally, and with compassion for yourself as you navigate this significant life transition.

PHASE Into Retirement™ is your guide for doing exactly that.

The Interconnection That Holds the PHASE™ Model Together

If retirement challenges people, it is rarely because one particular part of life falls apart. It is almost always because several parts shift simultaneously, creating a cascade of effects — some practical, some emotional, some invisible at first.

You leave work, and with it you lose:

- the structure of your days,
- the identity you wrapped yourself in for decades,
- the casual friendships born from proximity,
- the movement built into your routine,
- the mental engagement that came from problem-solving,
- the emotional reinforcement that comes from being needed.

Retirement doesn't remove one thread of your life — it removes an entire section of the tapestry. Without an intentional redesign, the rest of the fabric begins to sag.

This is why PHASE™ emphasizes interconnection. The five pillars do not function independently. They form a living ecosystem.

Purpose strengthens Health.

People with a sense of direction are more likely to move their bodies, stimulate their minds, and engage socially. Purpose fuels action, and action fuels vitality.

Health strengthens Activities.

When energy is high, when sleep is regulated, when mood is stable, people reach outward. They join classes, explore hobbies, and take on projects. When health declines, even enjoyable activities feel inaccessible.

Activities strengthen Social Life.

Most friendships in adulthood form around shared tasks. When retirees engage in activities — hiking groups, art classes, volunteer teams — connection happens naturally. Activities create proximity, repetition, and shared purpose, the three ingredients of friendship.

Social Life strengthens Everyday Routines.

People with active social calendars naturally develop rhythms. They get up earlier, move more, plan ahead, prepare meals, maintain self-care. Social connection is the heartbeat that drives routine.

Everyday Life strengthens Purpose.

Daily anchors — morning rituals, weekly rhythms, recurring commitments — reinforce identity. They remind you of what you value and why you get up in the morning.

These interconnections are not theoretical. They are observable in retirees everywhere.

Take someone who begins volunteering twice a week. They suddenly have reasons to wake up early, people to see, tasks to complete, and a sense of usefulness that boosts mood. Their physical health improves because they're moving more. Their mental health improves because they are contributing. Their social life expands because they meet others in the same cause. Their identity shifts from "former accountant" to "mentor, helper, organizer, friend." One choice began the cascade.

This is the power of the PHASE™ ecosystem: the whole is far greater than its parts. Change one dimension and the others start to shift in response. Sometimes subtly. Sometimes dramatically. When the ecosystem weakens, **t**he reverse is also true. When one pillar weakens, the others begin to strain. A decline in health limits mobility, which reduces activities, which shrinks social life, which stifles purpose, which disrupts routine. A lack of structure leads to inactivity, which weakens health, which limits activities, which increases isolation, which erodes purpose.

This is why retirees who don't proactively design their non-financial life often describe feeling "off" without knowing exactly why. It's not one thing — it's the subtle erosion across several parts of life.

Why interconnection matters for pre-retirees.

Understanding these interconnections before you retire is a tremendous advantage. It shifts your thinking from "What will I do?" to "Who will I become?" and "How will the pieces of my life sustain one another?"

If retirement is a redesign, interconnection is the blueprint.

Why interconnection matters for retirees.

For those already in retirement, recognizing the interdependence of the PHASE™ pillars provides clarity. It reveals why certain patterns feel so heavy, and why small changes can produce large improvements. When you strengthen one pillar, you begin to strengthen the system that supports all the others.

Interconnection transforms retirement from a puzzle into a living organism. It gives you leverage. It gives you agency. It shows you where to begin.

In the chapters ahead, you will explore each pillar in depth. But always keep the ecosystem in mind. Retirement is not a single decision — it is a series of interconnected choices that collectively shape a meaningful life.

P — Purpose

Reimagining Who You Are When Work No Longer Defines You

Purpose is often described as a compass, a north star, a guiding light. But in retirement, purpose is less poetic and far more practical. It is the force that moves you from bed to world, from idea to action, from thought to meaning. Purpose is not mystical. It is the way you answer two essential questions every day:

Who am I now?
How do I want to spend my time in a way that feels meaningful?

During working years, these questions rarely need your attention. Work answers them for you. Your role, your responsibilities, your routines, and the expectations placed upon you provide a built-in sense of direction. Even if you didn't always love your job, it structured your identity and offered definition: this is where I go, this is what I do, this is how I matter.

Retirement removes that scaffolding in a single afternoon. For some, the removal brings relief. For others, a sudden vacuum. For most, a mixture of both: freedom blended with disorientation.

A fulfilling retirement comes from intentionally rebuilding purpose, not as a replica of work, but as an expression of who you are becoming.

Purpose in retirement rarely looks like the purpose of your career. It is quieter, more self-directed, more reflective. It is shaped less by external validation and more by internal alignment. But it is no less powerful.

You can think of purpose as the emotional and psychological foundation of your new life. When it's strong, everything else becomes easier — health behaviors feel worthwhile, activities come alive, friendships deepen, and routines begin to flow naturally. When purpose weakens, life tends to flatten: motivation drops, engagement fades, routines slip, and the day feels like something to get through rather than something to participate in.

Purpose is not just meaningful; it is stabilizing.

The Identity Shift: Letting Go of the Work-Centered Self

The transition away from a work-centered identity is one of the most underappreciated emotional challenges of retirement. People expect to feel free, and they do — but that freedom often reveals how deeply their identity was entwined with their professional role.

Job titles function as shorthand for who we are. "I'm an engineer." "I'm a teacher." "I run a business." These statements carry weight. They signal competence, belonging, and contribution. They tell the world something about your value. They tell *you* something about your value.

When that shorthand disappears, the question "Who am I?" becomes more open-ended than many people expect. And open-ended questions, while liberating, are also unsettling.

This is why retirees often report feeling:

- Less confident
- Less relevant
- Less certain about how to use time
- Less connected to the world outside their home
- Less visible

These feelings are not signs of failure. They are signs of transition. Retirement requires a psychological recalibration — a shift from externally defined identity to internally created identity.

That shift doesn't happen automatically. It happens through reflection, experimentation, exploration, and the steady rebuilding of meaning.

What Purpose Looks Like in Retirement

Purpose in retirement is diverse, flexible, and deeply personal. It may include:

- A cause you care about
- A person you support
- A project you pursue
- A creative practice you develop

- A set of values you live out

- A role you inhabit in your family or community

- A curiosity you explore

- A routine that brings out your best self

Purpose is not measured by productivity. It is measured by resonance — a sense that your actions align with what matters most to you.

Some retirees find purpose in mentoring. Others in caring for grandchildren. Others in traveling, creating, volunteering, learning, or supporting their communities. Still others find purpose in personal growth — becoming healthier, more spiritually grounded, or more connected.

What matters is not *what* you choose, but **that you choose** — and that your choice is rooted in authenticity rather than expectation.

The Risks of a Purpose Gap

When retirees don't intentionally cultivate purpose, several predictable patterns emerge.

1. **Drifting:** Days feel interchangeable. Mornings lack urgency. Time expands but does not deepen.

2. **Emotional Flatness:** Without direction, many retirees feel dulled — not depressed, exactly, but muted. The spark that once drove them dims.

3. **Loss of Confidence:** Purpose is tied to identity. When you stop seeing yourself as someone who contributes, confidence begins to erode.

4. **Social Withdrawal:** People without purpose tend to withdraw, not because they want isolation, but because they lack the energy or direction to initiate connection.

5. **A Decline in Health Behaviors:** Purpose fuels action. When purpose fades, movement decreases, sleep becomes irregular, and nutrition patterns slip.

6. **Increased Rumination:** When the mind lacks outward focus, it often turns inward — not always helpfully. Worry, self-doubt, and rumination increase.

Again: none of this is a sign of failure. It is simply what happens when a central psychological need — meaning — goes unmet.

The opposite is also true: even a small sense of purpose can reverse these patterns.

The Benefits of Purposeful Living in Retirement

Purpose is a protective factor — emotionally, physically, and cognitively.

Research repeatedly shows that older adults with a strong sense of purpose:

- Live longer
- Recover faster from illness
- Experience lower levels of depression
- Maintain sharper cognitive functioning
- Report higher satisfaction with life
- Stay more socially connected
- Show greater resilience after loss or change

Purpose infuses life with vitality. It creates a sense of forward motion — a feeling that the next day holds something meaningful, something worth waking up for.

Purpose is not always loud. Often it is quiet but steady, like the hum of an engine under the hood. You may not always notice it in the moment, but it's what keeps you moving.

Building Purpose Before Retirement

Three years before retirement — sometimes more, sometimes less — is an ideal time to begin reshaping your identity and experimenting with new forms of meaning.

This period is not about reinvention; it is about exploration.

Reflecting on Values: Begin with questions that uncover what truly matters:

- What principles have guided my life so far?
- What qualities do I admire in myself at my best?
- What do I want more of in my life moving forward?

- What do I want less of?

Values are the roots of purpose. When you understand your values, you naturally gravitate toward activities and roles that align with them.

Exploring Identity Beyond Work: Most people have passions that drifted to the background during their career. Ask:

- What did I love doing before work consumed so much of my time?
- What interests have I ignored for decades?
- What have I always wanted to learn?

These dormant interests are not trivial. They are clues — reminders of who you were before work shaped your days.

Testing New Roles: Purpose is discovered through action.

Try small versions of what might become part of your retirement identity:

- Volunteer once a month
- Mentor someone
- Join a community advisory board
- Teach a class
- Join a committee or a service group
- Experiment with a creative pursuit
- Participate in a hobby or activity group

These micro-experiences reveal what energizes you and what drains you. They help you understand the difference between what sounds meaningful and what actually feels meaningful.

Redefining Success: During your career, success was measured externally — by performance, output, income, or recognition. In retirement, success must be measured internally — by alignment, joy, connection, and personal truth.

This shift requires practice. It requires letting go of the compulsive need to "produce" in order to feel worthy.

Crafting a Purpose Statement: A purpose statement is not a slogan. It is a brief articulation of who you are becoming.

For example: "I am someone who grows, contributes, and connects. I use my experience to help others, care for my community, and stay physically and mentally active."

Or: "I am a learner, a helper, and a creator. My purpose is to stay curious, stay connected, and stay engaged with the world around me."

Purpose statements give shape to your future self. They become a compass for decisions, routines, and relationships.

Rebuilding Purpose After Retirement

If you have already retired and feel even a slight sense of drift, know this: purpose can be rebuilt at any time. People in their 60s, 70s, 80s, and 90s have found renewed meaning through connection, learning, contribution, creativity, and service.

Beginning with the Present Tense: Avoid defining yourself by what you *used* to be. Instead of "I was…" Shift to "I am…" or "I am becoming…" Language is powerful. It reshapes perception. When you speak in the present tense, you bring your identity into the present rather than the past.

Following the Sparks: Purpose rarely arrives as a sudden revelation. It often begins as a spark — a moment of energy, curiosity, or joy.

Pay attention to:

- Topics that fascinate you
- Activities that leave you feeling more energized than when you started
- Conversations that linger in your mind
- People who draw out your best self
- Moments where you feel deeply present

Follow those sparks, even if you don't know where they lead.

Rebuilding Community: Identity does not grow in isolation. It grows through interaction. Joining groups, attending classes, and participating in community events provide mirrors — people who reflect back your strengths and contributions.

Designing Purposeful Routines: Purpose is strengthened by repetition. A weekly volunteer role. A daily writing practice. A monthly mentoring session. These recurring commitments deepen identity through consistency.

Staying Adaptive: Purpose is not static. It will evolve as your life evolves. Staying open to change protects against stagnation and allows purpose to grow with you.

Stories of Purpose in Action

Purpose can take many forms. Here are a few possibilities:

The Retired Engineer Who Became a Mentor: After 40 years in engineering, one retiree found purpose mentoring high school robotics teams. He said, "I thought I was going to miss being needed. Now I'm needed more than ever."

The Nurse Who Rediscovered Creativity: A former nurse took up pottery. What began as a hobby became a small business and a source of joy, grounding, and friendship.

The Executive Who Found Purpose in Caregiving: A corporate executive became the primary caregiver for his aging mother. He described it as "the most meaningful work I've ever done."

The Teacher Who Became a Lifelong Learner: A retired teacher joined a community book club and began writing essays. "I didn't leave education," she said. "I just changed roles."

Purpose does not require applause. It simply requires alignment.

Summary: Purpose as the Foundation

Purpose is the first pillar of PHASE™ for a reason: it animates every other dimension. Purpose gives shape to your identity, energy to your routines, meaning to your activities, and depth to your relationships. It transforms retirement from a phase of withdrawal into a phase of conscious living.

You do not need a grand mission. You only need **meaningful direction**. Purpose is not found. It is formed — piece by piece, choice by choice, day by day.

In the next chapter, you will explore Health — the energy source that allows purpose to flourish.

H — Health

Building the Physical, Mental, and Emotional Foundation for a Thriving Retirement

If Purpose is the compass that gives direction to retirement, **Health is the engine** that allows you to follow that direction. It is the quiet, often invisible force that determines whether your retirement feels expansive or restricted, joyful or burdensome, vibrant or diminished.

Health in retirement is not simply the absence of illness. It is the presence of energy. It is the ability to move through your days with clarity, confidence, and mobility. It is the emotional steadiness that helps you adapt to change. It is the mental vitality that keeps you learning, engaging, remembering, and reacting. It is the resilience that helps you navigate the unexpected.

Health touches every part of the PHASE™ ecosystem. When Health is strong, Purpose feels attainable, Activities feel enjoyable, Social Life feels accessible, and Everyday Life flows more easily. When Health falters, everything else becomes heavier.

Many people preparing for retirement imagine that health is something they will "get to later." They assume that once work slows down, they will finally make time for exercise, nutritious meals, stress reduction, better sleep, and mental well-being. But the transition into retirement often brings surprises. Without the structured routines of work, people actually move *less*. Without scheduled days, sleep patterns become irregular. Without the daily calls, projects, and interactions that kept the mind sharp, cognitive engagement decreases.

Retirement can be a flourishing period of energy and vigor — **if** health is strengthened intentionally. It does not require perfection, but it does require attention.

Health is the most powerful predictor of retirement satisfaction. It is also the most malleable: small changes compound into significant gains, even late in life. Your body is designed to adapt. Your brain is wired to grow. Your emotional system is capable of healing and strengthening well into your 70s, 80s, and beyond.

Retirement is not the time to slow down. It is the time to **shift your approach to health — from reactive to proactive, from accidental to intentional, from incidental to integrated.**

The Four Dimensions of Health in Retirement

Retirement requires a broader definition of health — one that reflects not just physical function but total well-being. PHASE™ defines Health across four interwoven dimensions:

1. **Physical Health:** Strength, balance, endurance, mobility, nutrition, sleep, preventive care.

2. **Mental Health:** Stress management, emotional regulation, clarity, mood stability, cognitive engagement.

3. **Emotional Health:** Resilience, optimism, adaptability, self-awareness, confidence.

4. **Cognitive Health:** Memory, attention, learning, neuroplasticity — the brain's ability to grow and adapt.

These dimensions interact. A daily walk improves physical health; it also boosts mood, stimulates the brain, regulates sleep, and provides social exposure. Reducing stress lowers inflammation and improves cognitive clarity. Learning something new stimulates the hippocampus, which improves memory and emotional regulation.

Health is a system. Everything affects everything.

The Hidden Health Risks of Retirement

People often imagine retirement as a health opportunity — a time to exercise more, sleep better, eat healthier, and create a lifestyle that supports wellness. In reality, retirement can create new risks if you don't prepare for the shifts that naturally occur.

1. **Decline in Movement:** Work provides movement you don't notice — walking between meetings, moving through hallways, climbing stairs, commuting, carrying materials, engaging in spontaneous physical tasks. Retirement removes those layers of incidental activity. Without intentional effort, daily movement drops substantially.

Less movement leads to:

- Muscle loss
- Reduced balance
- Stiffness
- Slower metabolism
- Weight gain
- Higher risk of chronic disease

2. **Irregular Sleep Patterns:** Without morning obligations, people often drift into later bedtimes and inconsistent wake times. Sleep becomes fragmented. The circadian rhythm loses its anchor, leading to:

- Mood instability
- Decreased cognitive performance
- Higher inflammation
- Lower energy

3. **Reduced Social Interaction:** Work relationships may diminish quickly. Isolation increases. And isolation, according to numerous studies, is as damaging to physical health as smoking or obesity.

4. **Increased Sedentary Time:** The average retiree sits 2–3 more hours per day than they did while working. Sedentary behavior increases risks for:

- Diabetes
- Cardiovascular disease
- Depression
- Joint problems
- Cognitive decline

5. **Stress Resurfacing Rather Than Dissolving:** Some retirees expect stress to disappear once work ends. Instead, stress may shift — from job demands to unstructured time, health concerns, caregiving needs, relationship changes, or identity loss. Stress becomes diffuse rather than focused, and therefore harder to identify or manage.

6.   **Mental Understimulation:** Work challenges your brain constantly: solving problems, managing interpersonal dynamics, adjusting to new information. Retirement requires you to build new opportunities for mental engagement or risk cognitive drift.

7.   **Emotional Disorientation:** Without structure, identity, and external validation, many retirees experience emotional heaviness, anxiety, or low motivation. This isn't a flaw — it's an expected part of a major life transition.

8.   **Increased Rumination:** When the mind is underchallenged, it turns inward. Rumination increases. Worry fills the space once occupied by tasks. Emotional health becomes harder to stabilize without the scaffolding of purpose and structure.

These risks are real — but they are absolutely preventable. And prevention begins with awareness, intention, and small, consistent behaviors.

The Benefits of Prioritizing Health

Retirees who invest in their physical, mental, emotional, and cognitive health experience transformations that are often dramatic — and deeply satisfying.

1.   **Increased Energy and Motivation:** Healthy behaviors create upward spirals. When you move more, sleep better, and feel more physically stable, your desire to engage with the world increases.

2.   **Improved Cognitive Function:** Learning new skills, reading, puzzles, language studies, and social interactions all stimulate neuroplasticity — your brain's capacity to grow. Retirees who pursue mentally stimulating activities maintain sharper memory and slower cognitive decline.

3.   **Better Emotional Stability:** Exercise, connection, sleep, and purpose regulate mood. Healthy retirees report fewer emotional swings, less stress, and more optimism.

4.   **Better Physical Function and Independence:** Strength and balance training maintain independence far into older age. Mobility becomes a source of confidence.

5.   **Greater Social Engagement:** Health creates capacity for connection. When you feel strong and energetic, you show up more often — and social life naturally expands.

6. **Increased Longevity and Reduced Disease Risk:** Daily movement, nutrition, and stress reduction dramatically reduce risks for heart disease, stroke, diabetes, and cognitive decline. Retirees who maintain healthy habits live longer, but more importantly — they live *better*.

7. **Enhanced Sense of Purpose:** When your body and mind feel good, you're more likely to seek out meaningful engagements. Health fuels purpose. Purpose fuels health.

   This virtuous cycle is one of the most powerful forces in retirement.

Building Health Before Retirement

Three years before retirement is the ideal time to begin strengthening health routines. You are still inside a structured lifestyle, and new habits integrate more naturally when anchored to an existing routine.

Here are the foundations:

1. **Daily Movement:** Daily movement does not mean intense exercise. It means consistency.

   - Walking
   - Stretching
   - Yoga
   - Light jogging
   - Swimming
   - Cycling
   - Strength training

   Your body interprets consistency as care.

   A 20-minute walk each day builds more long-term health than an intense workout done irregularly.

2. **Strength Training:** Muscle mass begins declining in your 30s and accelerates after age 50 — unless you actively rebuild it. Strength training is the most important physical habit you can build before retirement.

Strength equals independence.
Strength equals confidence.
Strength equals mobility.
Strength equals injury prevention.

Even two days a week will change your trajectory.

3. **Sleep Stabilization:** Before you lose your alarm clock, strengthen your circadian rhythm. Go to bed at the same time each night. Wake at the same time each morning. Protect the last hour of your evening — dim lights, quiet activities, low stimulation.

    A strong sleep pattern now will protect against drift later.

4. **Stress Management:** Stress does not disappear after retirement — it simply shifts its shape. Build emotional regulation tools now:

    - Mindfulness
    - Journaling
    - Breathing exercises
    - Nature walks
    - Gratitude rituals
    - Counseling or coaching if needed

    These tools will serve you long after your final workday.

5. **Mental Challenge:** Begin practicing intellectual hobbies:

    - Reading
    - Writing
    - Learning new skills
    - Taking classes
    - Doing puzzles
    - Learning instruments or languages

    Your brain thrives on challenge.

6. **Nutrition Foundations:** Retirement won't magically improve eating habits. Begin developing patterns of consistent meals, balanced nutrition, hydration, and reduced processed foods.

   Small shifts now create a steady baseline for later.

Rebuilding Health After Retirement

If you've already retired and find your health drifting, this is not a crisis — this is an opportunity. Behavioral science shows that new habits can be built at any age.

1. **Start Small and Start Now:** The biggest barrier to health is thinking you must start big. You don't. Start tiny:

   - Five minutes of stretching

   - A slow walk down the street

   - Drinking two more glasses of water

   - A consistent bedtime

   - A 10-minute brain game

   - A quiet moment of reflection

   Small habits accumulate. They activate identity: "I am someone who takes care of myself."

2. **Create Anchored Routines:** Anchor health behaviors to existing routines:

   - Stretch after brushing your teeth
   - Walk after breakfast
   - Read before bed
   - Practice balance exercises while waiting for the kettle to boil

   Anchored habits stick.

3. **Combine Movement with Social Life:** Walk with a friend. Join a fitness class. Participate in pickleball, hiking groups, or community exercise programs. Social accountability makes healthy routines easier and more enjoyable.

4. **Practice Emotional Hygiene:** You cared for your physical hygiene your whole life — brushing teeth, showering, grooming. Emotional hygiene is just as important:

    - Notice feelings without judgment
    - Ask for support when needed
    - Allow yourself time to adjust
    - Practice self-compassion

    Retirement is a major transition; grace is essential.

5. **Build Cognitive Routines:** Challenge your brain daily:

    - Learn something
    - Teach something
    - Discuss ideas
    - Play strategy games
    - Create something artistic

    Your brain does not want comfort; it wants stimulation.

6. **Schedule Preventive Care:** Don't wait for health problems to appear. Make preventive appointments part of your routine:

    - Annual physicals
    - Vision checks
    - Dental care
    - Vaccinations
    - Screenings

    Prevention is easier than recovery.

The Emotional and Psychological Side of Health

When people think of health, they often think of physical strength or cardiovascular fitness. But emotional health is equally important — and more closely tied to retirement success than many realize.

1. **Resilience Is Built, Not Inherited:** Resilience is not toughness. It is flexibility.

    It is the ability to bend rather than break, adapt rather than resist, learn rather than retreat. When retirees develop emotional resilience, they navigate changes with confidence rather than fear.

2. **Optimism Can Be Cultivated:** Optimism is not blind positivity. It is a trained habit of noticing possibility rather than limitation. Optimistic retirees are more likely to stay socially engaged and physically active.

3. **Self-Compassion Is a Strength:** Retirement brings mistakes, imperfect habits, and unexpected emotions. Responding to yourself with compassion — not criticism — is one of the most powerful health practices you can cultivate.

4. **Identity Affects Health:** If you see yourself as someone who is "aging," you behave differently than someone who sees themselves as "growing." Identity shapes behavior.

The Energy of a Healthy Retirement

When retirees strengthen their health across physical, mental, emotional, and cognitive dimensions, a profound shift occurs:

- Energy rises
- Motivation returns
- Curiosity reawakens
- Social life expands
- Purpose deepens
- Structure becomes easier

Health unlocks possibility.

Health gives retirement its vitality.

Health transforms years into life.

A — Activities

The Engagement, Curiosity, and Creativity That Bring Retirement to Life

When most people imagine retirement during their working years, their minds leap to images of rest — long mornings, slow afternoons, coffee on the porch, a gentle ease settling into the day. For a while, rest feels exactly like the reward it's supposed to be. The body exhales. The mind unclenches. The calendar stops yelling.

But soon enough, an unexpected truth reveals itself: **rest is wonderful, but only in contrast to engagement.** Without engagement, rest becomes something else — lethargy. And lethargy is not rest at all. It is drift.

The retirees who describe their lives as vibrant, full, exciting, meaningful, or satisfying are rarely the ones who "rested" the most. They are the ones who engaged the most — with hobbies, interests, passions, curiosities, crafts, causes, classes, challenges, and communities. They are the ones who used retirement not to withdraw, but to rediscover and rebuild the parts of themselves that work pushed to the margins.

Activities are not filler. They are the architecture of a meaningful day. They give texture to time. They give you something to anticipate, something to practice, something to improve at, something to share, and often something to laugh about. They are the glue that holds the emotional, cognitive, and social dimensions of retirement together.

Activities are not a luxury. They are a necessity — one of the most powerful predictors of whether retirement becomes a chapter of joy or a slow slide into boredom and isolation.

Why Activities Matter More Than Most People Realize

A hobby is not a hobby. At least, not in the casual sense of the word. What we casually refer to as "hobbies" are, in reality, the primary drivers of psychological well-being in later life. They meet three essential human needs:

Autonomy — the freedom to choose what you do

Mastery — the satisfaction of getting better at something
Connection — the relationships formed through shared interests

When these needs go unmet, retirement becomes hollow. When they are met, retirement becomes joyful.

Activities tap into something primal — our innate desire to create, to learn, to explore, to improve, and to belong. These desires do not disappear with age. They simply get buried under obligation. When work ends, the dirt is cleared away. What grows next is up to you.

People often misunderstand activities as "time fillers." This could not be further from the truth. Activities are the experiences that give your days purpose, your brain stimulation, your body movement, and your relationships depth. They are the antidotes to isolation, boredom, anxiety, and the "now what?" feeling that haunts many early retirees.

Without engaging activities, time becomes an enemy. With them, time becomes a gift.

The Quiet Danger of Having No Activities

The danger of an activity-free retirement isn't dramatic. It doesn't show up immediately. It shows up slowly, quietly, subtly — in the ways days start blending together, in the diminishing spark of excitement, in the feeling of being "out of sync" with the world.

Without meaningful activities, retirees often describe:

- boredom that feels heavier than expected

- restlessness that has no place to go

- lack of motivation to get out of the house

- reduced movement, reducing health

- fewer social interactions

- increased rumination

- sleep patterns that drift

- a sense of shrinking rather than expanding

This is not a weakness of character. It is a natural human response to the loss of external engagement. The brain craves stimulation. The mood craves novelty. The body craves movement. The spirit craves expression.

Without these outlets, the emotional texture of life dulls. Gratitude fades. Enthusiasm thins. Even joyful events feel muted.

The good news is this: the slide into disengagement is reversible. It is reversible at 60, 70, 80, even 90. The human brain retains neuroplasticity throughout life. It is always capable of learning, adapting, and forming new patterns.

But it needs stimulation. And stimulation comes from activity.

The Rich Benefits of an Engaged Retirement

Retirees who regularly engage in meaningful activities describe an entirely different emotional reality than those who do not. Their days have shape. Their weeks have rhythm. Their minds are active. Their bodies are moving. Their relationships are vibrant. Their purpose is reinforced.

Activities provide:

Mental vitality. Learning new skills stimulates neural growth, strengthens memory, and improves cognitive flexibility. Creative activities light up the brain.

Emotional stability. Engagement lifts mood, reduces anxiety, and provides a buffer against depression.

Social connection. Activities lead naturally to friendships. People bond through doing far more easily than through small talk.

Physical health. Even light physical activities — gardening, dancing, walking — improve balance, strength, mobility, and cardiovascular health.

Renewed identity. Hobbies help retirees reshape who they are becoming. A former accountant becomes a photographer. A nurse becomes a potter. An executive becomes a gardener.

Structure. Activities create natural anchors in the week — classes, rehearsals, meetups, projects, and community commitments.

Forward motion. Activities give the day a sense of beginning, middle, and end — and life a sense of unfolding, growing, and becoming.

Activities provide the "why" behind getting up in the morning.

The Science Behind Engagement and Why It Matters

A growing body of research confirms what many retirees intuitively sense: engagement is life-giving. Longitudinal studies across the United States, Canada, Japan, and Europe reveal powerful patterns.

Retirees who actively pursue hobbies are:

- significantly less likely to report depression
- more likely to rate their health as "good" or "excellent"
- more likely to maintain cognitive performance
- more likely to stay socially involved
- significantly more likely to describe retirement as "thriving" rather than "enduring"

Active leisure — hobbies that involve participation rather than passivity — produces measurable psychological benefits. Brain imaging studies show that creative and social activities enhance neural pathways, particularly in the prefrontal cortex and hippocampus, regions responsible for memory, decision-making, and emotional regulation.

Creative engagement — music, writing, painting, woodworking, crafting — triggers dopamine release, which enhances motivation and joy.

Physical engagement — gardening, dancing, hiking, exercise — improves cardiovascular function and reduces inflammation.

Social engagement — clubs, classes, volunteer work — increases oxytocin and serotonin, which regulate mood and connection.

Hobbies aren't entertainment. They're medicine.

Why Building Activities Before Retirement Matters

The three years before retirement provide an ideal window for testing, experimenting, and building the habits that will sustain you in the next chapter. This period is psychologically significant. It allows you to explore new interests while still having the structure of work to stabilize your life.

Rediscovering Curiosity

Start by noticing what sparks your interest. Pay attention to moments of "I've always wanted to try that." Those moments are valuable clues.

Maybe it's woodworking. Maybe it's painting. Maybe it's foreign languages. Maybe it's hiking. Maybe it's music. Maybe it's restoring furniture. Maybe it's volunteering with kids or animals. Maybe it's cooking. Maybe it's learning about local history. Maybe it's joining a choir.

Let curiosity lead.

Testing Interests in Low-Stakes Ways

Avoid the temptation to fully commit before experimenting. Sign up for a short class rather than a yearlong program. Rent equipment before buying it. Visit a group before joining it. Give yourself permission to walk away if it's not a match.

You're not looking for a life-defining passion. You're looking for glimmers of engagement — the small sparks that can grow into something meaningful.

Building Future Social Circles

Engagement is not just about the hobby itself. It's about the people you meet along the way. Join groups tied to your interests. Show up consistently. These small actions create the early bonds that can blossom into post-retirement friendships.

Creating the Conditions for Mastery

Mastery does not require expertise. It requires practice. And practice requires time. Retirement gives you that time — but it helps to start early. When retirees begin building skills before they retire, they enter their next chapter with confidence and momentum.

Letting Go of Perfectionism

Many professionals unconsciously carry their work mindset into their hobbies — expecting proficiency, productivity, or perfection. But the healthiest retirees approach activities with playfulness. They embrace being beginners again. They treat activities as opportunities for joy, not evaluation.

How to Build Activities After Retirement

If you have already retired and feel like your days have become too quiet, too still, or too repetitive, this is not a crisis — it is a starting point. Engagement can be built from scratch at any age.

Start with One Small Activity

Choose something simple: a weekly class, a monthly meetup, a daily creative practice, or a slow exploration of something you've long been curious about. The first step is not about intensity; it's about momentum.

Follow What Feels Energizing

Pay attention to anything that makes you feel even a little lighter. Enthusiasm is a compass. If you leave an activity feeling more alive, lean into it.

Join Groups, Not Just Activities

Joining a group transforms a solo interest into a social connection. Even introverts benefit from gentle, low-pressure group experiences. Book clubs, walking groups, community education classes, choirs, photography meetups — these settings create a natural social rhythm.

Allow Activities to Evolve

A hobby may begin as something quiet and individual but evolve into something communal or purposeful. A gardener may join a community garden. A reader may lead a book discussion. A woodworker may teach beginners. A volunteer may become a leader in a nonprofit.

Leave room for evolution. Retirement is long. Interests shift. Passions emerge. Let life grow.

Share What You Love

One of the most meaningful transitions retirees experience is the shift from participation to contribution. Teaching, mentoring, demonstrating, presenting, helping others learn —

these forms of contribution deepen identity, strengthen relationships, and amplify purpose.

People who share their hobbies often discover a richer version of the activity itself.

Let Communities Adopt You

Many retirees underestimate how eager communities are to welcome new members — particularly those with time, curiosity, and life experience. Whether it's a church group, a volunteer organization, a museum docent program, or a local sports club, communities thrive on participation. They are waiting for people like you.

Examples of Activities That Transform Retirement

The Golfer Who Became a Naturalist

A retiree began golfing four days a week, enjoying the leisure at first. But soon the routine felt empty. One morning he noticed the birds along the fairway and began identifying them. Within months, he had joined a birding group, taken field trips with naturalists, and become a volunteer guide for local school groups. His days feel fuller now — not because of golf, but because the curiosity sparked by golf turned into something richer.

The Former Accountant Turned Woodworker

After decades of numerical precision, one retiree found relief in working with his hands. He built small furniture pieces for friends, then for a community charity auction. Today he teaches a beginner's woodworking class at the local community center. "I thought I'd miss work," he says. "Turns out I found something better."

The Retired Nurse Who Rediscovered Music

Music had always been part of her youth, but work left no room for it. Two years into retirement, she joined a community choir. She describes it as "the thing that gives my week a pulse."

The Executive Who Became a Volunteer Reading Mentor

After retiring, he realized he missed feeling useful. He signed up to tutor children once a week. Three years later, he's a cornerstone volunteer in the program. "They need me," he says, "and I need them."

Activities are rarely accidental. They are invitations — small moments of interest that grow into life-giving practices.

The Psychology of Engagement

Activities are powerful because they satisfy psychological needs that work once fulfilled.

They create structure.

A class at 10 a.m. or a rehearsal on Thursday night adds shape to the week.

They sustain identity.

Hobbies become part of who you are. "I paint." "I hike." "I volunteer." These statements rebuild confidence.

They expand community.

Activities bring people together repeatedly — and repetition builds trust.

They reduce rumination.

Engagement pulls your attention outward, reducing worry and mental spinning.

They spark growth.

The brain thrives on novelty and challenge.

They anchor purpose.

Activities often lead to contributions that feel meaningful.

The Activity Portfolio: Depth and Breadth

A fulfilling retirement typically includes a mix of:

- physical activities
- creative or intellectual activities
- social activities
- service or contribution-based activities

This blend creates balance, resilience, and variety. You don't need dozens of hobbies — just a few that make you feel engaged and alive.

When Activities Become Meaning

Activities often begin as leisure and become purpose. The gardener becomes the neighborhood horticulture helper. The painter begins donating art to charity events. The reader becomes a literacy volunteer. The hiker becomes a trail steward. The traveler becomes a cultural storyteller.

In this way, activities become bridges — from interest to identity, from curiosity to contribution.

Summary: Activities Are the Lifeblood of a Meaningful Retirement

Retirement is long. It can be filled with life or drained of it — and the difference often comes down to activities.

Activities:

- stimulate your mind
- strengthen your body
- deepen your relationships
- increase your motivation
- give your days rhythm

- nourish your identity

- expand your purpose

A fulfilling retirement is not built in the abstract. It is built through the daily, weekly, and monthly experiences that bring joy, curiosity, meaning, and connection.

Activities are not side notes.

They are the story itself.

S — Social Life

Connection, Belonging, and the Friendships That Shape a Joyful Retirement

If health is the engine of a thriving retirement and purpose is the compass, then **social life is the heartbeat** — the rhythmic, steady pulse that keeps the rest of life warm, vibrant, and human. Friendship and connection matter more to retirement well-being than almost any other factor. The science on this is overwhelming: social isolation increases mortality risk more than obesity, and loneliness is as physiologically harmful as smoking fifteen cigarettes a day.

Retirement intensifies this truth. For decades, your work life supported your social life. You interacted with colleagues, clients, customers, students, vendors, partners, and peers. You shared stories, frustrations, successes, challenges, meetings, and meals. You talked at the coffee machine. You checked in at the start of meetings. You problem-solved together. You celebrated wins. You shared the strain of difficult days.

Work did more than pay the bills. It gave you a community.

When work ends, that community dissolves faster than most people expect. Not because people don't care. Not because the relationships were shallow. But because work friendships are held together by proximity and shared purpose — two forces that evaporate the moment your last day ends.

This is not a personal failure. It is a natural shift. But it is a shift most retirees are unprepared for. And if left unaddressed, it becomes one of the quietest and most painful challenges of retirement: the slow, surprising disappearance of connection.

But the reverse is equally true: if cultivated intentionally, social life becomes one of the greatest joys of retirement — a source of laughter, meaning, belonging, motivation, and emotional health.

The Difference Between Work Friends and Life Friends

People often underestimate how much their adult friendships come from work. Work is one of the last environments in life where people see each other regularly, repeatedly, and with shared goals. These three ingredients — proximity, repetition, and purpose — form the foundation of friendship.

When work ends, these ingredients disappear. And relationships that were sustained by context rather than personal investment often fade away.

Work friends are:

- convenient
- consistent
- tied to common goals
- built on shared experiences

But once the common environment disappears, so does the ease of connection.

Life friends, however, operate differently. They are chosen, not assigned. They endure transitions because they are built on shared values, interests, humor, trust, or history. Life friends don't require a conference room or a common task to stay connected.

Retirement is a shift from work friendships to life friendships. It is a shift from proximity-based relationships to intention-based relationships.

This is why retirees benefit immensely from cultivating **non-work, non-family** friendships before retirement arrives. These friendships are more durable, more resonant, and more aligned with your values and interests — because you chose them, not because work placed you together.

Why Social Life Matters So Deeply in Retirement

Social life is not simply about having people to do things with. It is about having people to be *yourself* with.

Healthy social connection provides:

Belonging: A psychological sense of fitting in, being known, and being valued.

Visibility: The feeling that someone sees you — and that your presence matters.

Emotional Support: People who will listen, celebrate, comfort, and encourage.

Cognitive Stimulation: Conversations that challenge your thinking and keep your mind sharp.

Physical Health Benefits: Better cardiovascular function, lower inflammation, stronger immunity, longer lifespan.

Motivation: Connection encourages movement, structure, purpose, and engagement.

Identity Reinforcement: Friends remind you who you are — and who you are becoming.

Without these benefits, retirement becomes a quieter, smaller place.

The Risks of Social Shrinkage

Retirement often brings an unintended shrinking of the social world. It begins subtly — fewer conversations, fewer shared projects, fewer moments of "How are you?" and "You won't believe what happened yesterday."

Left unchecked, this shrinkage can lead to:

- **Isolation**

  Days pass without meaningful interaction.

- **Loneliness**

  A painful sense of separation from others — even if people are technically nearby.

- **Depression**

  Mood declines when human connection fades.

- **Anxiety**

  The world feels less predictable and more overwhelming.

- **Cognitive Decline**

  Social interaction stimulates the brain; without it, cognitive agility weakens.

- **Loss of identity**

  Without people reflecting your strengths and stories back to you, identity blurs.

- **Physical health decline**

  People move less, eat worse, and sleep irregularly when isolated.

This slide does not happen all at once. It happens one skipped invitation at a time. One quiet week at a time. One "I'll call them later" that turns into months. One retreat into comfort that becomes a habit.

The antidote is not simply "being more social." The antidote is intentionally rebuilding a **social ecosystem**.

The Social Ecosystem of a Healthy Retirement

A thriving social life in retirement is not built on one or two people. It is built on **layers** — a diverse, steady ecosystem that keeps you engaged, connected, and supported.

This ecosystem includes:

Close friends: A small group — often 3 to 8 people — with whom you share trust, honesty, and emotional closeness.

Activity-based friends: People you see regularly through classes, clubs, volunteer work, or hobbies.

Community circles: Groups, congregations, teams, or communities where you are known and welcomed.

Acquaintances: The barista who knows your name, the neighbor you chat with, the regulars at the gym or walking trail.

Family: Children, siblings, relatives — but family cannot fulfill all social needs alone.

Each layer provides something important:

- Close friends provide depth.

- Activity friends provide consistency.
- Community groups provide belonging.
- Acquaintances provide lightness and casual interaction.
- Family provides continuity and care.

A strong social ecosystem includes all five layers.

When retirees lack this ecosystem, social life becomes fragile. When one relationship ends — through conflict, distance, illness, or death — they may be left without backup support. But retirees with a diverse ecosystem are resilient. They have multiple sources of connection, energy, and belonging.

Building Social Life Before Retirement

The best time to build your retirement social ecosystem is **three years before you retire**. This timeframe allows new friendships to form naturally while you still have the structure of work supporting your routine.

Starting with Awareness

Begin by taking inventory of your current relationships:

- How many of your friendships are tied to work?
- How many extend beyond it?
- Which relationships energize you?
- Which ones drain you?
- Where do you feel known and seen?

Awareness is the first step. You cannot build what you have not identified.

Expanding Your Circles

Start joining groups or communities that have nothing to do with work:

- a local club
- a community class

- a volunteer organization
- a sports or activity group
- a book club
- a faith community
- a travel group
- a neighborhood association

The goal is not to force friendships. The goal is to place yourself in environments where friendships can grow through repetition and shared experience.

Showing Up Consistently

Friendships don't form because of one great conversation. They form because of **repeated exposure**. People need to see you often enough to become comfortable. This is where many adults falter — they attend once or twice, then stop.

Consistency is the secret ingredient.

Investing in a Few Emerging Relationships

Notice the people you naturally gravitate toward. The ones who make you feel at ease. The ones who ask good questions. The ones who share your humor or your interests. These are the seedlings of friendship.

Nurture them through small gestures — a coffee invitation, a shared walk, an offer to help.

Letting Yourself Be Known

Relationship depth requires vulnerability. This does not mean sharing your life story all at once. It means letting people see a little more of who you are — your interests, your challenges, your values.

People connect with authenticity, not perfection.

Rebuilding Social Life After Retirement

If you are already retired and feel your social life shrinking or stagnating, remember this: **it is never too late to build connection**. Humans are wired for community. That wiring does not degrade with age.

Start Small and Local

Begin with the people closest to your daily environment:

- neighbors
- regulars at the gym
- people walking their dogs
- people in your building or community center

Small daily interactions plant seeds.

Join Activity-Based Groups

Activity-based groups are especially powerful in retirement because they provide structure and shared purpose:

- hiking clubs
- volunteer teams
- writing groups
- art classes
- music ensembles
- gardening collectives
- pickleball leagues
- travel groups

Shared activity creates natural rapport.

Volunteer Regularly

Volunteering is one of the most reliable pathways to meaningful connection in later life. Shared service creates deep bonds — and it invites a sense of purpose that strengthens the PHASE™ ecosystem.

Host Micro-Gatherings

People often assume gatherings must be elaborate. They do not. Invite two or three people for coffee, a walk, or a casual meal. Small is intimate. Small is manageable. Small builds trust.

Create Recurring Rituals

A monthly dinner. A weekly walking group. A Thursday morning coffee at the same café. Rituals are the backbone of connection. They add rhythm to your week and reliability to your relationships.

Say Yes More Often

When someone invites you — even casually — say yes more than you say no. Connection requires openness. The more often you step into social spaces, the easier they become.

Why Social Life Must Be Built Intentionally

People often resist intentionality in social life because it feels forced, or because they imagine friendships must happen "organically." But organic friendship is rare in adulthood because proximity shrinks. You no longer see the same people every day. Your life is less structured. Your social exposure decreases.

Friendship in adulthood is not spontaneous. It is built through:

- repetition
- shared experiences
- effort
- vulnerability

- reciprocity

- patience

There is nothing artificial about intentional friendship. It is simply adulthood's version of organic childhood friendship — slower, steadier, more deliberate, and more deeply rewarding.

The Social Life Paradox

Many retirees discover a paradox: the more isolated they feel, the harder it becomes to reach out. Isolation creates inertia. And inertia is powerful.

This creates a self-reinforcing cycle:

- You stop seeing people → social skills rust

- Social skills rust → social environments feel intimidating

- Social environments feel intimidating → you avoid them

- You avoid them → you become more isolated

Breaking this cycle requires one small act of courage — the willingness to step toward people, even when it feels uncomfortable.

Once the cycle breaks, connection returns more quickly than most retirees expect.

The Emotional Rewards of Friendship in Retirement

Healthy friendships in retirement offer emotional benefits that ripple through the rest of life:

Laughter

Retirees with strong social circles laugh more often. Laughter reduces stress hormones, supports immune function, and increases emotional resilience.

Belonging

Belonging gives life its warmth. It satisfies one of the deepest human needs.

Support in Hard Times

Retirement brings challenges — caregiving, health issues, loss. Social support softens these edges.

Shared Joy

Good news is better when shared. Success multiplies. Joy expands through connection.

Identity Reinforcement

Friends remind you of who you are. They reflect your strengths back to you.

Meaning and Purpose

Connection gives life meaning. It anchors your place in the world.

Stories of Social Renewal

The Former Sales Manager Who Felt Lost

Within six months of retiring, he felt invisible. He joined a morning walking group after seeing a flyer at the community center. Within weeks, he had friends. Within months, he had purpose again.

The Retired Teacher Who Started a Monthly Dinner Club

She began inviting neighbors — some she barely knew — for simple meals. Today, the club is in its eighth year.

The Widower Who Finally Said Yes

After his wife's death, he withdrew. His daughter encouraged him to join a gardening club.

He resisted — until he didn't. Now he spends three mornings a week with people who have become like family.

The Newcomer to Town

A couple relocated to be closer to grandchildren. They joined a volunteer reading program. They now have a community of friends that rival any they had earlier in life.

Social life in retirement is not passive. It is built. And what you build can become one of the richest sources of joy in your later years.

Summary: Social Life Is the Heartbeat of Retirement

Social connection is not optional. It is essential. It determines:

- how joyful your days feel
- how healthy your body stays
- how sharp your mind remains
- how grounded your identity is
- how resilient you are in hard times
- how meaningful your retirement becomes

Friendship is not a luxury of retirement — it is the lifeblood of it.

Retirement may remove the social scaffolding of work, but it presents an extraordinary opportunity: the chance to build an entirely new social life based on choice, values, and shared joy rather than obligation.

You are not meant to face retirement alone. You are meant to live it among people who bring out your best, challenge your thinking, and walk alongside you in the years to come.

Your next chapter is not defined by how many people you know — but by how deeply you are connected to the people who matter.

In the final PHASE™ pillar, you will explore Everyday Life — the structure and rhythm that give retirement its grounding, stability, and momentum.

E — Everyday Life

The Rhythm, Stability, and Structure That Keep Retirement Grounded

Everyday Life — the structure and rhythm of your days — is the quiet backbone of a fulfilling retirement. It doesn't call attention to itself the way Purpose does. It doesn't generate the excitement of Activities or the warmth of Social Life. It doesn't carry the urgency of Health. Yet without structure, even the most carefully cultivated purposes, hobbies, friendships, and health routines begin to fray.

Everyday Life is where all the other parts of the PHASE™ ecosystem are actually lived out. Structure is not glamorous, but it is transformative. It turns intentions into habits, and habits into identity. It creates a sense of movement, order, and clarity that supports every dimension of your post-work life.

During your working years, structure is built into your days whether you want it or not. Your alarm clock rings. Your commute begins. Your meetings are scheduled. Your deadlines are imposed. Your breaks are predictable. Your mealtimes are squeezed into windows. Your evenings revolve around the demands of the next morning. This rhythm may not always feel comfortable, but it is reliable.

When work ends, that external scaffolding disappears overnight. What remains is a wide-open expanse of time — something that feels like freedom on the surface, but quickly becomes overwhelming if left unshaped.

Most new retirees underestimate the significance of this shift. They assume structure will build itself or that they'll naturally gravitate toward routines that support them. But time is not self-organizing. Left alone, it expands, dissolves, and rearranges itself in ways that erode motivation and emotional clarity.

The happiest retirees are not the busiest ones. They are the ones who build routines that give their days shape, reliability, and momentum — routines that align with their values, purpose, health, activities, and social life.

Structure is not about rigidity. It is about rhythm — a rhythm that supports your well-being, your growth, and your evolving sense of self.

Why Everyday Structure Matters So Much in Retirement

Structure provides several vital psychological and emotional benefits:

Predictability

Structure creates a sense of psychological safety. When you know what your day and week look like, your mind relaxes. Predictability reduces stress and supports emotional regulation.

Momentum

A structured day gets moving faster. When you begin with a grounding ritual, the rest of the day tends to follow with more energy and intention.

Identity Reinforcement

The things you do regularly become part of who you are. If your routines include movement, learning, contribution, and connection, your identity becomes anchored in those values.

Healthy Constraints

The right structure keeps unhealthy habits from creeping in — excessive screen time, irregular meals, inconsistent sleep, or sedentary routines.

Meaning-Making

Rituals turn ordinary moments into meaningful ones. A morning walk becomes meditation. A weekly lunch becomes connection. A monthly volunteer shift becomes purpose.

Without structure, retirement days blur. With structure, they come into focus.

What Happens When Structure Vanishes

One of the earliest and most common challenges retirees report is a feeling of disorientation. They may describe:

- waking up without urgency or direction
- drifting between tasks
- trouble maintaining consistent sleep
- irregular eating habits
- feeling unproductive even on relaxed days
- emotional heaviness
- a sense of shrinking motivation

This disorientation is not a personal failing. It is a natural response to the removal of external structure.

Some retirees stop setting an alarm entirely and wake whenever their body chooses. This feels liberating for a week or two, then slowly disrupts their circadian rhythm. They begin staying up later. Their mornings drift. Their routines scatter. They lose the sense of "start" that once set their day in motion.

Others find themselves aimlessly filling time with screens — TV, phones, tablets — not because they enjoy it, but because unstructured time seeks easy dopamine. Technology becomes the default, not the intention.

Others lose track of days entirely. Without the weekly cadence of meetings and deadlines, Monday feels like Thursday feels like Sunday. The week dissolves into a vague cycle.

Again: this is not failure. It is simply what happens when structure is not intentionally rebuilt.

The Psychological Importance of Routines

Humans are rhythmic creatures. We function best with patterns that repeat regularly. Rituals provide ground beneath our feet. They help us transition between states — from sleep to wakefulness, from morning to afternoon, from week to weekend.

Routines have outsized benefits:

They preserve cognitive clarity.

When your mind doesn't have to reinvent your day from scratch, it frees mental bandwidth for creativity, learning, and connection.

They strengthen healthy habits.

If a habit is tied to a routine, you don't rely on motivation alone to maintain it.

They reduce anxiety.

Predictable rituals calm the nervous system and reduce mental uncertainty.

They increase satisfaction.

Studies show that retirees with regular routines report higher overall life satisfaction.

They build identity.

You don't become active by thinking about walking. You become active by *walking every morning.*

The Power of a Morning Anchor

The single most important structural choice in a retiree's day is the **morning anchor** — the ritual that begins the day with intention and momentum. It doesn't need to be complicated. It doesn't need to be early. It simply needs to be consistent.

A morning anchor might include:

- a walk
- stretching
- reading
- meditation

- journaling
- making breakfast
- sitting outside
- reviewing intentions for the day

The anchor creates a boundary between night and day — a gentle but powerful signal to your mind that the day has begun.

Retirees who establish morning anchors often report:

- better mood
- improved energy
- more consistent sleep
- fewer sluggish mornings
- greater motivation to engage socially or physically

Without a morning anchor, the day often begins in a haze. With one, the day begins with clarity.

Weekly Rhythms: The Architecture of the Retirement Week

If mornings create daily structure, weekly rhythms give retirement its broader shape. Weekly rhythms create anticipation, order, and identity.

Examples include:

- Monday morning volunteer shift
- Tuesday walking group
- Wednesday afternoon class
- Thursday evening dinner with friends
- Friday morning hobbies
- Weekend family time
- A weekly household routine

The specifics don't matter. The rhythm does.

Without weekly rhythms, the week becomes unmoored. With them, life gains a pulse.

Building Structure Before Retirement

If you are still working, you have a significant advantage: your days already have a built-in rhythm. The goal in your pre-retirement phase is to begin layering intentional structures into your life so that when work ends, your days do not collapse into formlessness.

Identify the Structures You Want to Keep

Some routines already support you — your workout schedule, your reading habits, your family rituals. These are assets. Bring them with you into retirement.

Build Routines That Reflect Your Future Values

Start incorporating routines that support the life you want:

- healthy meals
- consistent sleep
- regular physical activity
- weekly social engagements
- purposeful tasks

These become the foundation of post-retirement life.

Create a Prototype Retirement Day

Once a month, live a "retirement day"—a day free from work structured only by your desired routines. These prototypes reveal what works and what needs adjustment.

Experiment with Weekly Rhythms

Begin building weekly rhythms now so that when work ends, these rhythms expand naturally into your new schedule.

Establish a Morning Anchor

Start now. It will be your stabilizer later.

Rebuilding Structure After Retirement

If you're already retired and feeling the drift, building structure is less about discipline and more about design.

Start with One Daily Ritual

Choose one anchor. Morning is ideal, but any consistent time works. Build your day around it.

Create One Weekly Commitment

A class. A volunteer shift. A walking group. One commitment creates a rhythm. Two create momentum. Three create a week.

Set Gentle Boundaries Around Time

Wake around the same time. Eat at consistent times. Limit late-night technology. Respect your sleep cycle.

Use the "Three Pillars Per Week" Approach

Every week, engage at least once in:

- something physical
- something social
- something mentally or creatively stimulating

These three pillars build structure naturally.

Honor the Boring but Important

Meals. Laundry. Bills. Cleaning. These routines create stability. They anchor your life in the practical world. They matter more than you think.

Review and Adjust Monthly

Your needs and interests will evolve. So should your routines. Review your rhythms monthly and adjust with curiosity rather than judgment.

The Emotional Power of Everyday Life

Structure does more than organize time. It organizes emotion.

It reduces anxiety.

When your days feel predictable, your nervous system settles.

It builds confidence.

When your routines align with your values, you feel more grounded in who you are.

It fosters gratitude.

Daily rituals reveal small joys — sunlight in the morning, coffee on the porch, familiar faces on your walking route.

It softens transitions.

Loss, change, health challenges, and life disruptions are inevitable. Structure softens the edges.

It reinforces identity.

Your routines become expressions of your values, shaping the person you become in retirement.

Retirees often underestimate how stabilizing simple routines can be — until they build them, and life becomes calmer, clearer, and richer.

Stories of Everyday Life in Action

The Former Executive Who Found Peace in a Morning Ritual

After decades of high-pressure work, he struggled with slow mornings. He began rising at the same time each day, making tea, sitting outside, and reading for 20 minutes. This simple ritual transformed his days.

The Couple Who Built a Weekly Social Calendar

They scheduled gentle rhythms — a Monday breakfast out, Wednesday pickleball, Friday dinner with neighbors. Their week now feels structured without feeling busy.

The Solo Retiree Who Battled Drifting

Living alone, he often drifted into long, unstructured days. He created a weekly template: movement in the morning, errands in the early afternoon, creative projects in the late afternoon. His mood and energy stabilized within weeks.

The Volunteer Who Found Her Week's Anchor

Her Thursday morning volunteer shift became the pillar of her week — something she looked forward to, prepared for, and built her other routines around.

Everyday Life is not glamorous, but it is quietly powerful.

Closing Summary:

Moving Forward with PHASE Into Retirement™

You have explored all five pillars of the PHASE™ framework: Purpose, Health, Activities, Social Life, and Everyday Life. Together, these dimensions shape the emotional, physical, psychological, and social reality of retirement.

Your PHASE™ results are not predictions. They are reflections — a snapshot of where you are now and a compass for where you'd like to go. They illuminate strengths. They highlight opportunities. They reveal imbalances. They point toward the next small step.

Retirement does not demand perfection. It asks for intention.

Here is what matters most as you move forward:

Build on what's strong.

Use your strengths as anchors. Let them support the parts of life that feel less stable.

Choose one area to strengthen next.

You don't need to change everything. You only need to begin somewhere.

Use the ecosystem to your advantage.

Strengthen one pillar, and the others will begin to rise with it.

Let purpose guide you.

A sense of meaning — however quiet or small — fuels momentum.

Let health energize you.

Your body and mind are capable of more than you imagine, even later in life.

Let activities excite you.

Follow your curiosity. Let hobbies evolve. Let learning continue.

Let relationships support you.

You are not meant to do this alone.

Let routines steady you.

Structure gives your days rhythm, predictability, and grounding.

Retirement is not the end of something.

It is the unfolding of a new chapter — a chapter shaped by your choices, your values, and your willingness to live with intention, curiosity, and connection.

PHASE™ Into Retirement™ gives you the framework.

You bring it to life.

Your next years can be among the richest, most meaningful, and most joyful you have ever lived — not by chance, but by design.

www.ingramcontent.com/pod-product-compliance
Lightning Source LLC
Chambersburg PA
CBHW081146160726
47997CB00020B/2792